Is it...?

Shiny or dull

Vic Parker

Heinemann
LIBRARY

Little Nippers

www.heinemann.co.uk/library
Visit our website to find out more information about **Heinemann Library** books.

To order:
☎ Phone 44 (0) 1865 888066
▤ Send a fax to 44 (0) 1865 314091
▯ Visit the Heinemann Bookshop at www.heinemann.co.uk/library to browse our catalogue and order online.

First published in Great Britain by Heinemann Library, Halley Court, Jordan Hill, Oxford OX2 8EJ, part of Harcourt Education.
Heinemann is a registered trademark of Harcourt Education Ltd.

Editorial: Jilly Attwood and Claire Throp
Design: Jo Hinton-Malivoire and bigtop, Bicester, UK
Models made by Jo Brooker
Picture Research: Rosie Garai and Sally Smith
Production: Séverine Ribierre

Originated by Dot Gradations
Printed and bound in China by South China Printing Company

ISBN 978 0 431 17401 3 (hardback)
08 07 06 05 04
10 9 8 7 6 5 4 3 2 1

ISBN 978 0 431 17406 8 (paperback)
08 07
10 9 8 7 6 5 4 3 2

British Library Cataloguing in Publication Data
Parker, Vic
Is it shiny or dull?
620.1'1295
A full catalogue record for this book is available from the British Library.

Acknowledgements
The publishers would like to thank Gareth Boden for permission to reproduce photographs.

Cover photograph reproduced with permission of Gareth Boden.

The publishers would like to thank Annie Davy for her assistance in the preparation of this book.

Every effort has been made to contact copyright holders of any material reproduced in this book. Any omissions will be rectified in subsequent printings if notice is given to the publishers.

The paper used to print this book comes from sustainable resources.

Contents

Time for a treasure hunt

This teacher wants to make a display of **shiny** and **dull** things.

What can the children find at home?

5

One dull spoon. One shiny spoon.

Blowing bubbles

Bubbles are shiny too.

Watch them waft away...

Stepping outside

I spy with my little eye, two dull things. Can you guess?

10

Flower pots and watering can!

11

Sprinkling and sparkling

Sand is dull ...

12

but **glitter** is **shiny**.

sparkle

sparkle

13

In the kitchen

Are these pasta shapes shiny?

Are these sweets dull?

Testing toys

Shiny cars – sleek and *speedy.*

Dull teddy – **soft** and **snuggly**.

17

ha ha!

Dirty old shoes!

19

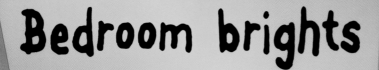

Bedroom brights

How many **shiny** things can you count?

They're great for dressing up!

Classroom display

Top marks for the treasure hunt.

dull things

shiny things

Index

The end

Notes for adults

The *Is it . . . ?* series provides young children with a first opportunity to examine and learn about common materials. The books follow a boy and girl as they go on a treasure hunt around their house to find items with contrasting textures. There are four titles in the series and when used together, the books will encourage children to express their curiosity and explore their environment. The following Early Learning Goals are relevant to this series:

Creative development
Early learning goals for exploring media and materials:
• explore colour, texture, shape, form and space in two or three dimensions
• begin to describe the texture of things.

Knowledge and understanding of the world
Early learning goals for exploration and investigation:
• investigate objects and materials by using all of their senses as appropriate
• show curiosity, observe and manipulate objects
• describe simple features of objects
• look closely at similarities, differences, patterns and change.

This book introduces the reader to a range of everyday items that are shiny or dull. It will extend young children's thinking about familiar objects and enable them to talk expressively about different materials. The book will help children extend their vocabulary, as they will hear new words such as *sleek* and *waft*. You may like to introduce and explain other new words yourself, such as *metal* and *cloth*.

Follow-up activities
• Collect some shiny sweet wrappers, sequins and glitter. Stick them on to paper to make a shiny collage.
• See how many objects your child can find that can be both shiny and dull. For instance: a shiny new coin and a dull old coin; a shiny pair of shoes and a dull pair of shoes, a shiny metal spoon and a dull wooden spoon. Then mix the objects up into a heap and play a 'sorting' game into 'dull' and 'shiny' piles.
• On a supermarket shopping trip, identify whether each object put into the trolley is shiny or dull.